FUN FOR
T·E·N · F·I·N·G·E·R·S

Easy pieces and puzzles for young pianists

PAULINE HALL AND PAUL DRAYTON

Second edition

Consultants: Janet Bullard and Jeanette Gallant

Illustrations: Rosie Brooks

Play-along audio tracks are available on major streaming platforms or to download from a companion website: www.oup.com/funforten

OXFORD
UNIVERSITY PRESS

Great Clarendon Street, Oxford OX2 6DP, England
This collection © Oxford University Press 1995 and 2025.
Unless marked otherwise, all pieces are by Paul Drayton. All pieces are © Oxford University Press.
Unauthorized arrangement or photocopying of this copyright material is ILLEGAL.
Pauline Hall and Paul Drayton have asserted their right under the Copyright,
Designs and Patents Act, 1988, to be identified as the Authors of this Work.
Impression: 1
ISBN: 978–0–19–357404–5
Music and text origination by Julia Bovee
Printed in Great Britain

Farmer

Cheerfully

Here's the farm - er mak - ing hay, she hopes the sun will shine all day. If it rains and

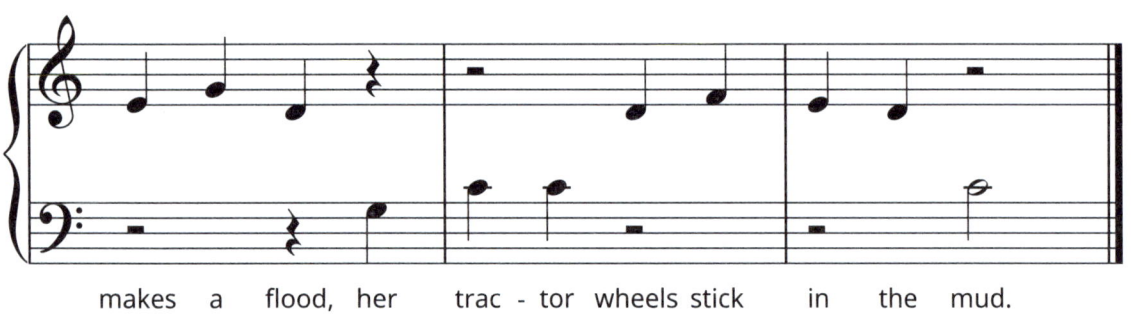

makes a flood, her trac - tor wheels stick in the mud.

Accompaniment

Engine driver

Look out for an F sharp.

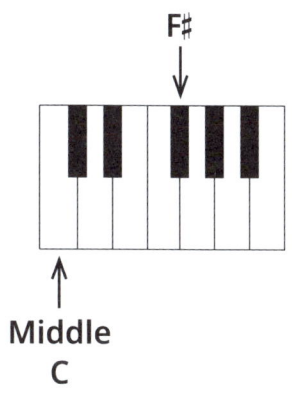

Speedily

Why not be an en-gine driv-er if you have the chance? Whiz-zing through the Chan-nel Tun-nel: next stop, France!

Accompaniment

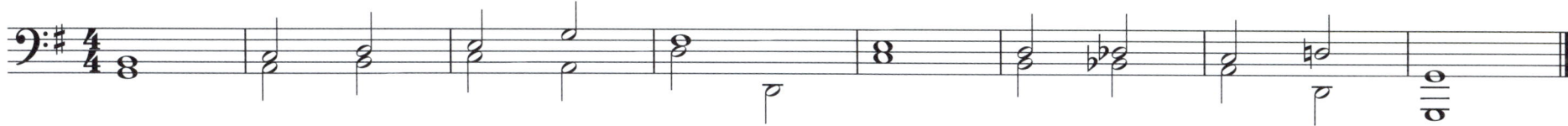

Astronaut

Look out for a B flat for your left hand!

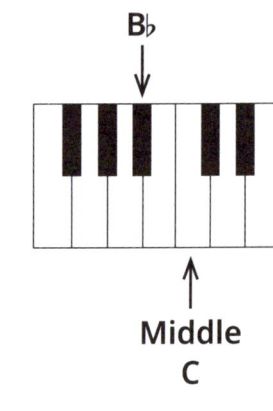

Floatingly

Mer-cur - y,   Ve -nus too,   Ju - pi - ter, and Mars: Fur-ther still,   in - to space,   e - ven to the stars.

Accompaniment

sempre arpegg.

Space (and lines too!)

Some of these notes are in spaces, and some of them are on lines.

Draw a circle around each space note, and join the line notes with a line.

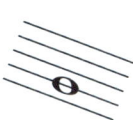

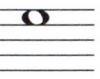

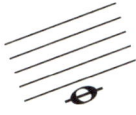

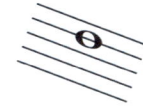

Ghost

Before you play, can you spot two B flats?

Spookily

I'm   the   ghost of   the   haunt - ed   house— I'll   try   to   give you   a   fright._____   As   long   as   I   ne - ver

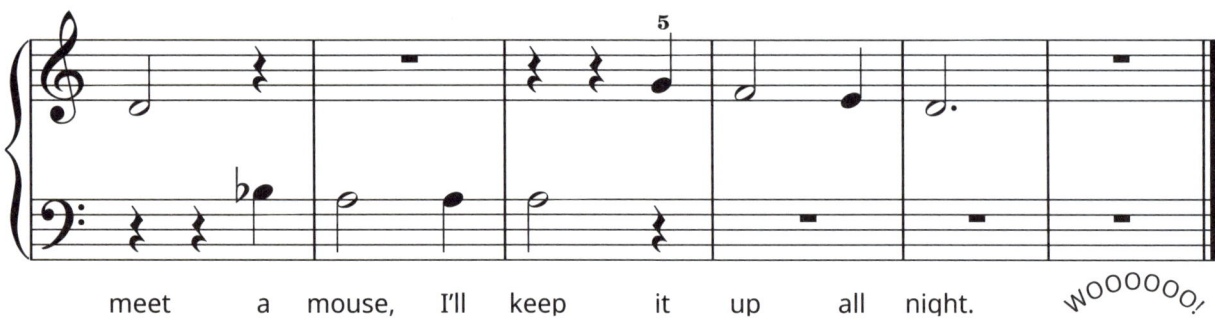

meet   a   mouse,   I'll   keep   it   up   all   night.   *WOOOOOO!*

Accompaniment

Make up your own ghost tune

First, put the right pedal down—it's called the **sustain** pedal.
If you can't reach, you may have to sit on the very edge of the piano stool, or stand up.

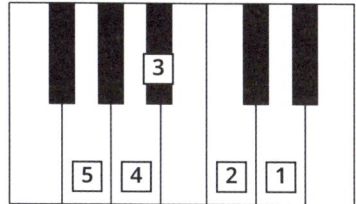

Then put your left hand over these five keys—choose a set low down at the end of the piano so that they will sound very deep and mysterious.

Play them in a clump all together as quietly as you can.

Put your right hand over these keys.

Play the notes in any order—very slowly and very quietly.
It must sound like a ghost creeping through the shadows.

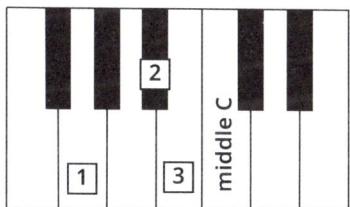

Try adding some extra notes. Keep the pedal pressed down all the time!

Postman

Here comes the post-man Joe, rid - ing through the rain and snow; carry - ing in his great big sack a

post-card sent by Un - cle Jack.

Accompaniment

Play and sing!

Are you a good listener? Can you remember things? Try this listening game.

Play this note:  Take it off and *think* the sound of it. Wait ... then sing it!

Play it again—was your singing note the same?

Try another 'listen and remember': 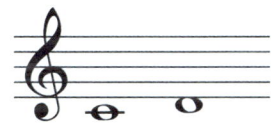 Wait while you remember, then sing the notes. Play them again to check.

Try some more 'play and sing' games—you'll get better at doing them!

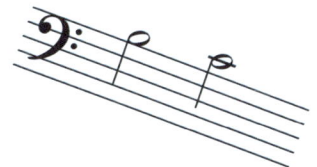 

Santa Claus

How many times does your right hand play F sharp in this tune?

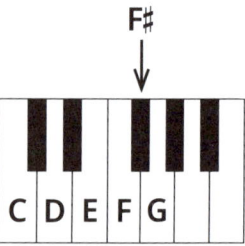

Spikily

San - ta Claus comes down the chim-ney look-ing ve - ry jol - ly. He sinks in - to a com-fy chair up - on a sprig of hol - ly!

Accompaniment

A Christmas carol

Traditional West country carol

Merrily

We wish you a mer-ry Christ-mas, we wish you a mer-ry Christ-mas, we wish you a mer-ry Christ-mas and a hap-py New

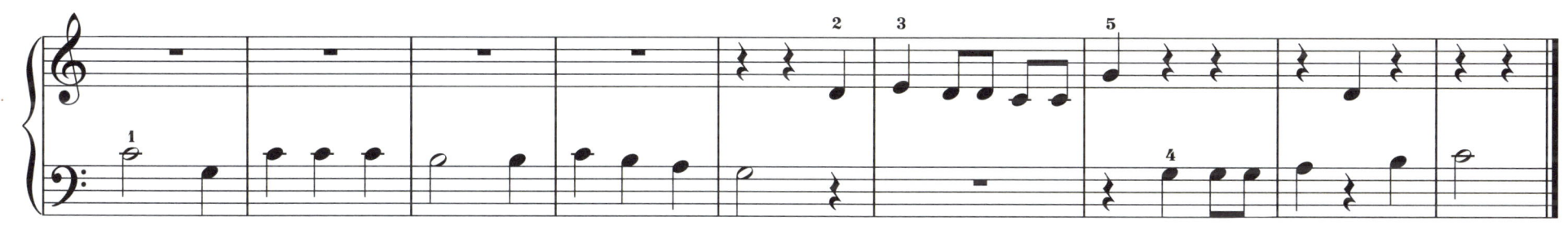

Year. Good ti-dings we bring to you and your kin; We wish you a mer-ry Christ-mas and a hap-py New Year!

Pirate

Breezily

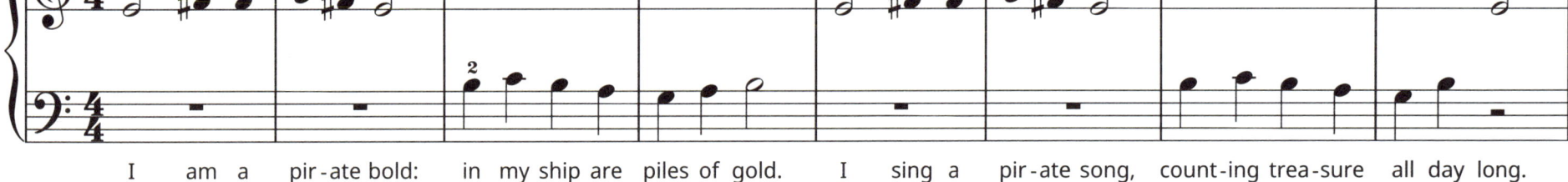

I am a pir-ate bold: in my ship are piles of gold. I sing a pir-ate song, count-ing trea-sure all day long.

Accompaniment

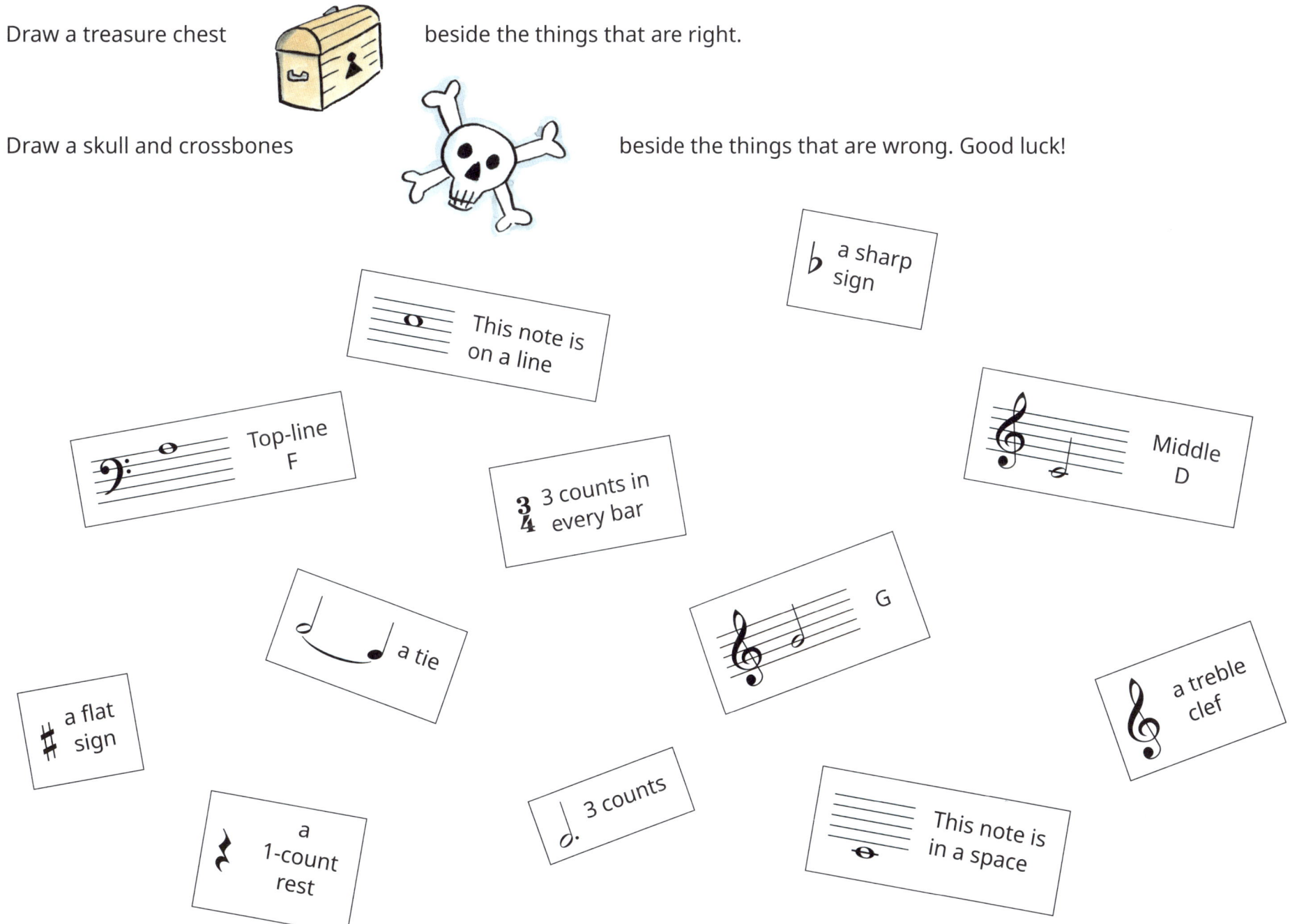

The pirates have found a cave with lots of things washed up from a sunken ship, but not all of them are treasure!

Draw a treasure chest beside the things that are right.

Draw a skull and crossbones beside the things that are wrong. Good luck!

a sharp sign

This note is on a line

Top-line F

3/4 3 counts in every bar

Middle D

a tie

G

a flat sign

a treble clef

a 1-count rest

3 counts

This note is in a space

Journalist

How many flats are there in this piece?

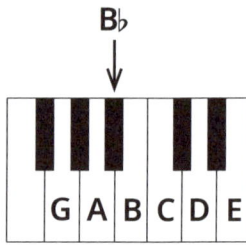

Watch as the T V jour - nal - ist brings all the ex - cit - ing news, A wea - ther re - port and

all the sport with some live - ly in - ter - views.

Accompaniment

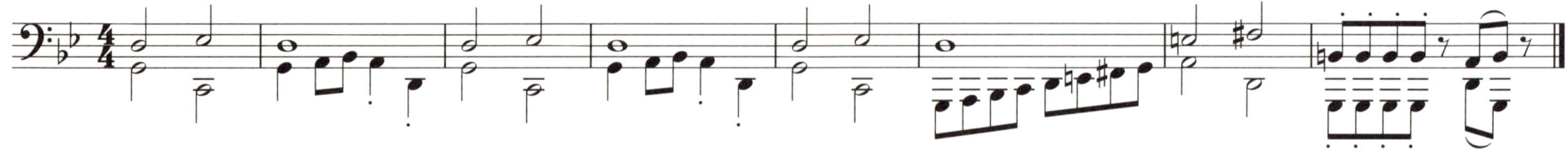

The journalist will often talk to other journalists in different countries.
Here are five of those countries, hidden as musical notes. Can you work out what they are?

Helper

Busily

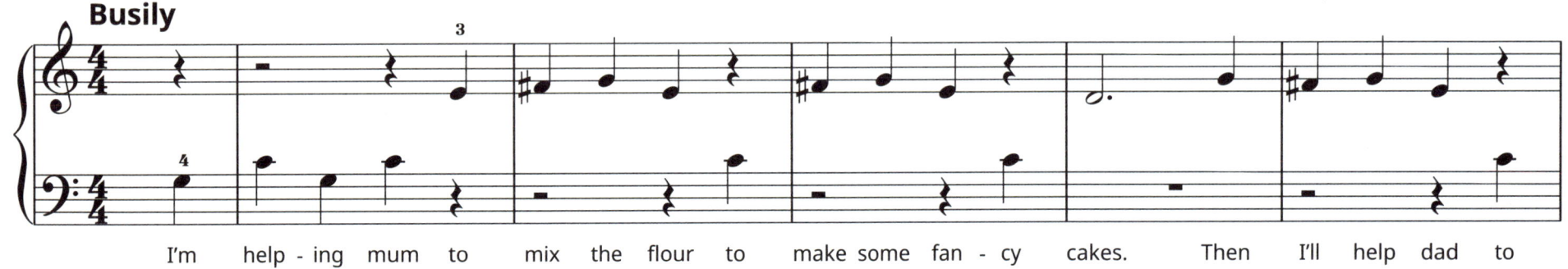

I'm help - ing mum to mix the flour to make some fan - cy cakes. Then I'll help dad to

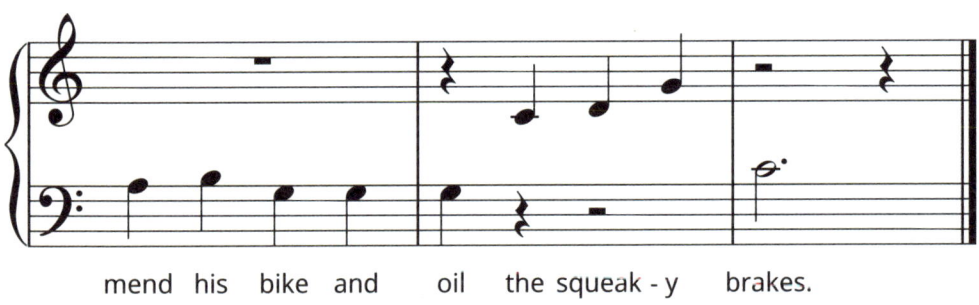

mend his bike and oil the squeak - y brakes.

Accompaniment

At the market

This is a game to play with someone else—perhaps your teacher.

At the market there are lots of baskets of fruit, but all the labels have fallen off. Can you help?

Take it in turns to clap a rhythm, then write the number on the label below each fruit.

1. 2. 3. 4. 5. 6. 7. 8.

Strawberry   Grapefruit   Oranges   Watermelon

Plum   Pineapple   Avocado   Cherries

18

Scarecrow

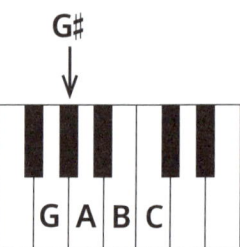

Lonely

Here in the field I stand all day, try-ing to keep the birds a - way.

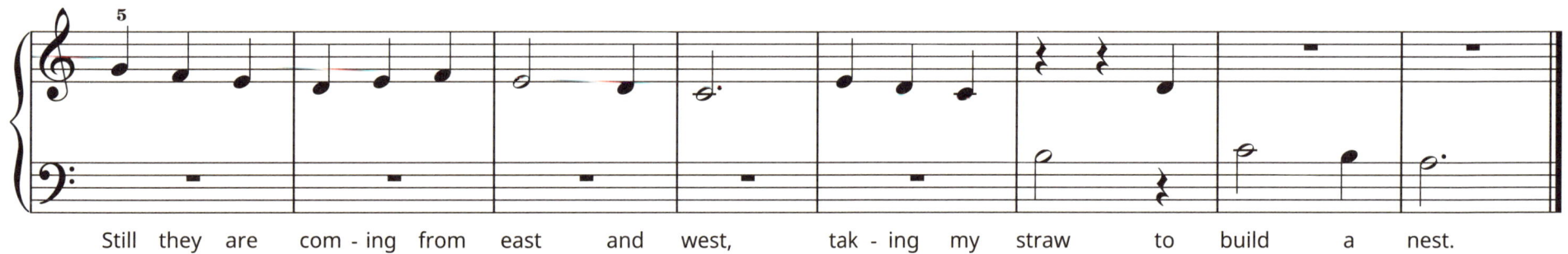

Still they are com-ing from east and west, tak-ing my straw to build a nest.

Accompaniment

Steps and skips

When you play next-door notes like this: 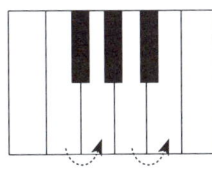 it's a STEP.

When you play two notes with one in between like this: 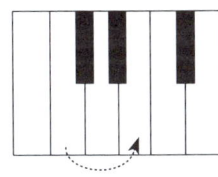 it's a SKIP.

Now for an adventure! Where will you end up?

Follow the instructions given for each hand below. You can use one finger, or more if you like.
Try not to look at the keyboard—feel your way if you're not sure where to go.

Right hand
Start on middle C, then go up a STEP, up a SKIP, up another SKIP, then down a STEP. Where did you land?

Left hand
Start on middle C, then go down a STEP, down a SKIP, up a STEP, then up a SKIP. Where did you land?

Try some more of your own, starting on different notes. Where did you get to?

Artist

I've sharp-ened all my pen-cils, so now what shall I draw? Aunt-ie Jane? Or a

bowl of fruit? Or Bon-zo the dog next door?

Accompaniment

Explorer

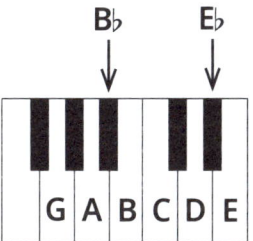

Stealthily

Deep in the trop - ic - al for - est there's so much for us to ex - plore; and we may

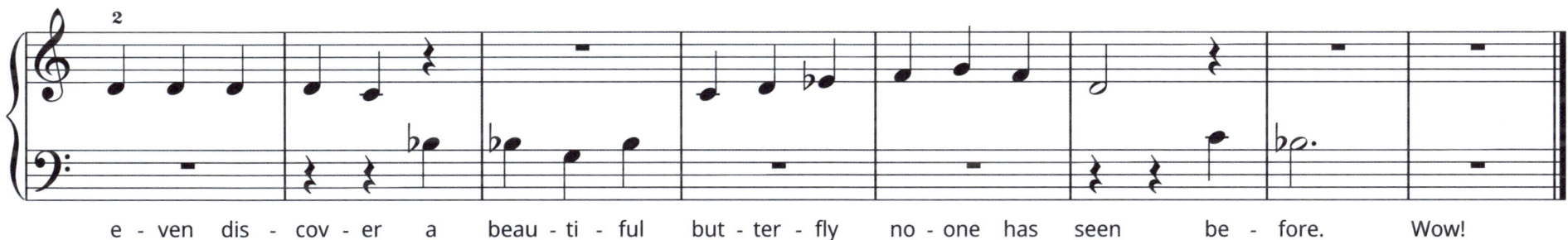

e - ven dis - cov - er a beau - ti - ful but - ter - fly no - one has seen be - fore. Wow!

Accompaniment

8va sempre

Footballer

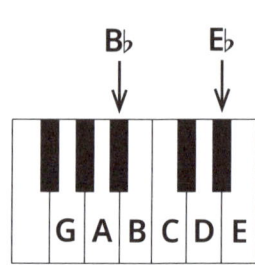

Keenly

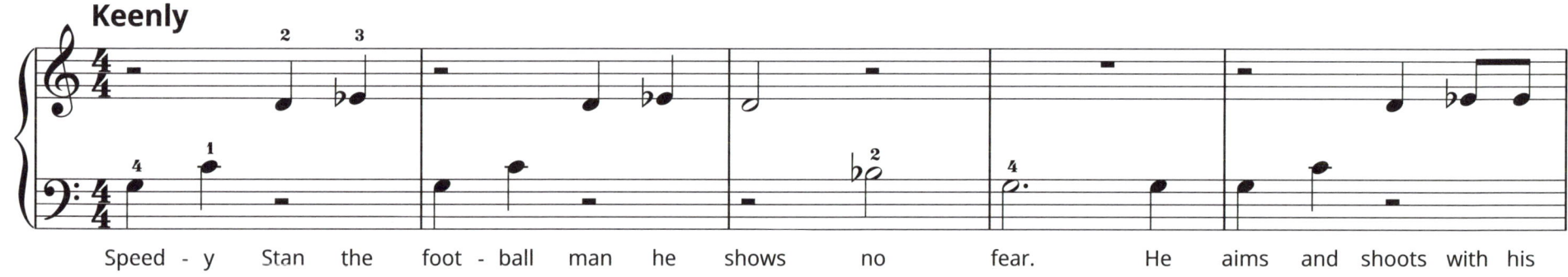

Speed-y Stan the foot-ball man he shows no fear. He aims and shoots with his

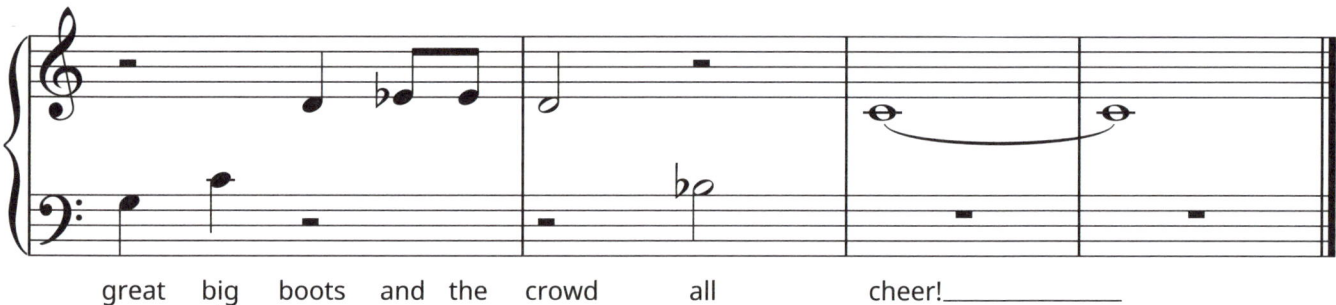

great big boots and the crowd all cheer!_____

Accompaniment

The top scorer

Beside every goal is the letter name of a note. If you can draw it on its own line or in its own space, you score!

The first one is done for you to show you how.

SCORE

Gymnast

B flat and A sharp share the same key.

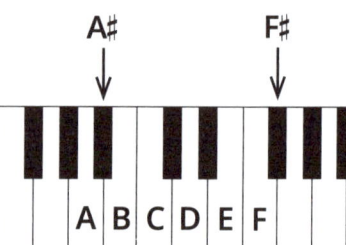

Bendily

Turn-ing cart-wheels on the beam, her bod-y's like e - las - tic. She's the best in all the team at a - ny-thing gym - nas - tic.

Accompaniment

Banjo player

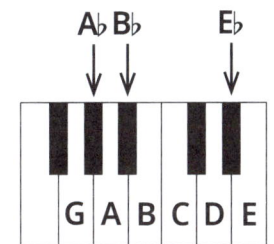

The ban-jo tune goes round and round: it makes a plin-ky, plon-ky sound. It

must be hard to know, I think, just when to plonk and when to plink!

Accompaniment

Magician

Look out for D flat in your right hand!

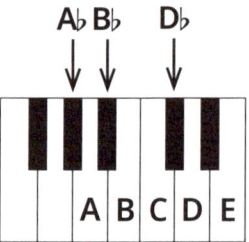

Have you seen the great ma-gi-cian make a pen-ny dis-ap-pear? Then he says the ma-gic word and

takes it out of some-one's ear!

Accompaniment

A magic trick for the piano

Can you make a note sound without actually playing it?

With your left hand, very slowly press five low-down keys so that they don't make a sound. Keep them held down. With your right hand, play a high-up key as loudly as you can (*ff*) and **staccato**.

Listen, what can you hear?

Try it again with some different notes. Did it work?

When the magician did his trick, what magic word did he say?

Write the letter names of the notes here:

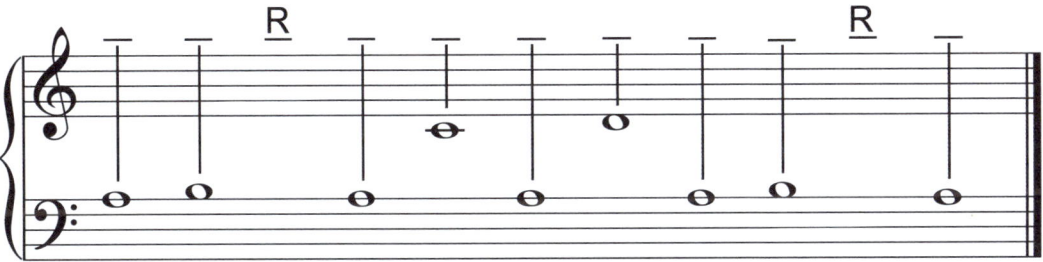

Cyclist

Energetically

One day I'll be a cyc-list in the O-lym-pic ve-lo-drome. Till then I'll have to ride my bike in the gar-den here at home.

Accompaniment

Zookeeper

Helpfully

So ma-ny jobs to be done in the zoo: feed-ing the lion and the kan - ga - roo,

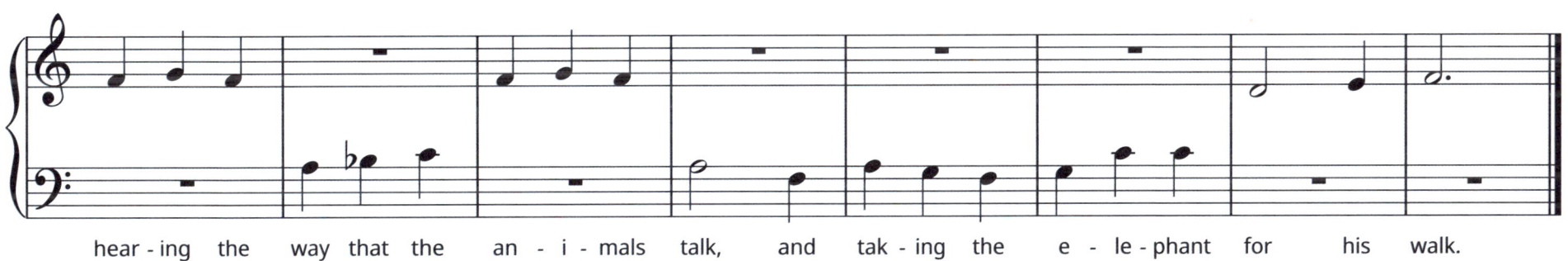

hear-ing the way that the an - i - mals talk, and tak-ing the e - le -phant for his walk.

Accompaniment

Gardener

There are lots of flat keys—two for each hand.

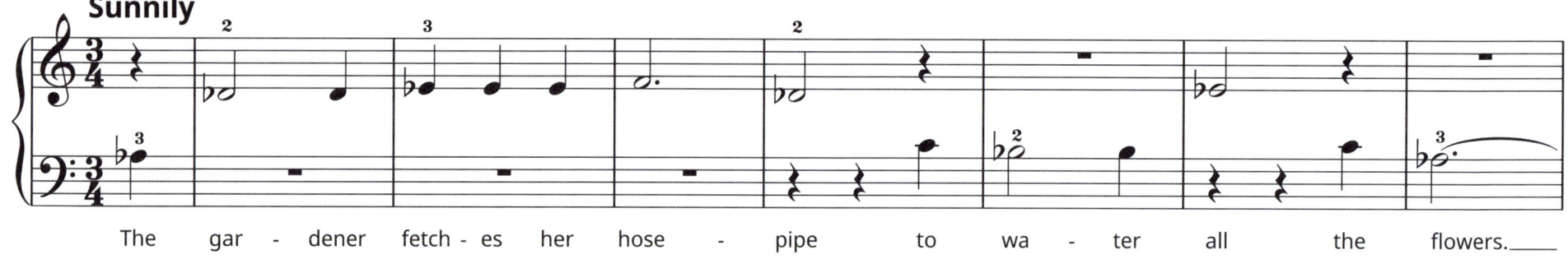

The gar - dener fetch - es her hose - pipe to wa - ter all the flowers.____

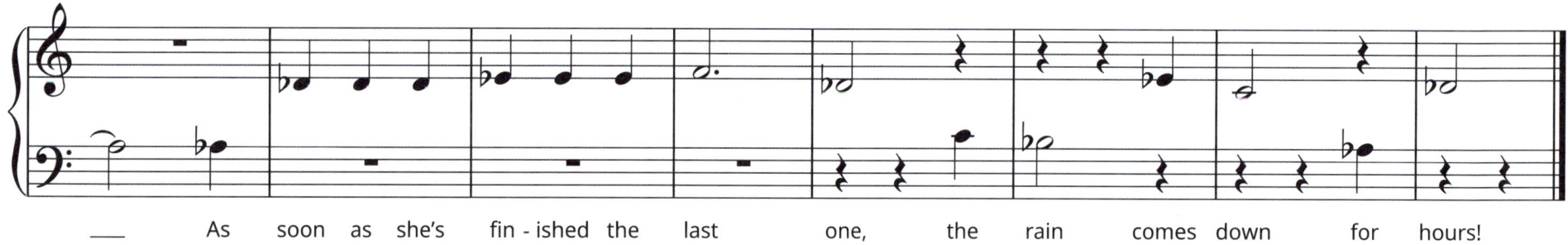

____ As soon as she's fin - ished the last one, the rain comes down for hours!

Accompaniment

What's happening in the garden?

All these flowers have somehow escaped from their flowerpots.
Clap their names, then write their numbers on the correct pots.

1. Bluebell   2. Rose   3. Daffodil   4. Honeysuckle

5. Water lily   6. Snapdragon   7. Lily-of-the-valley   8. Buttercup

Snooker player

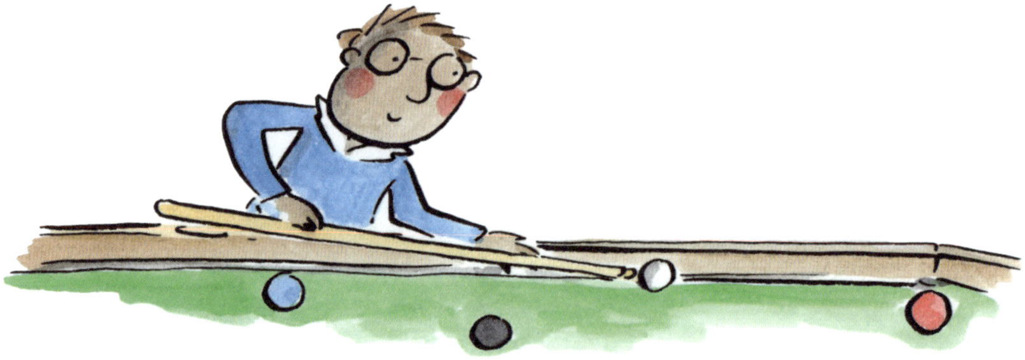

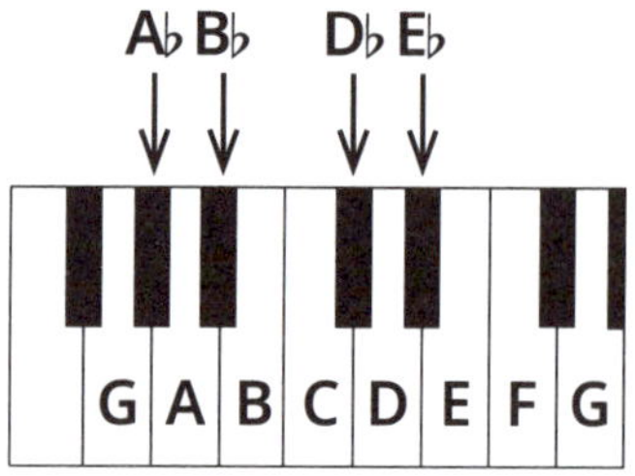
A♭ B♭ D♭ E♭
G A B C D E F G

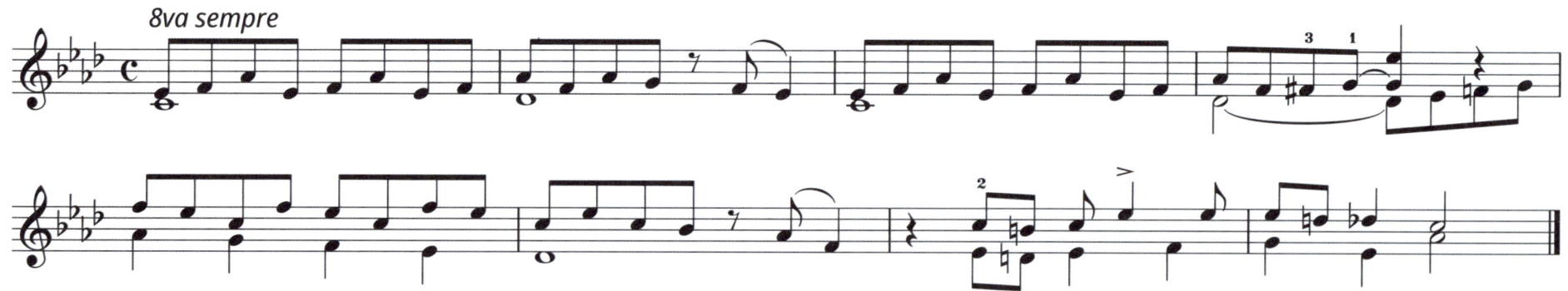

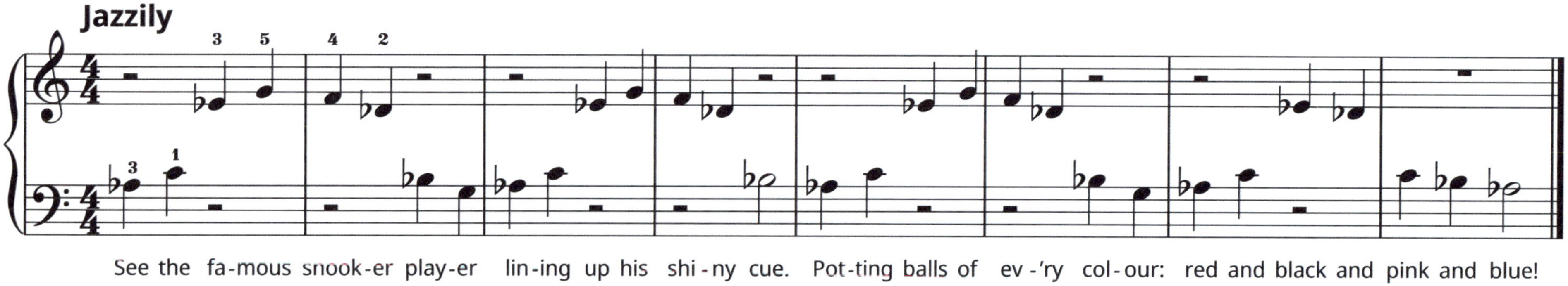
Jazzily
See the fa-mous snook-er play-er lin-ing up his shi-ny cue. Pot-ting balls of ev-'ry col-our: red and black and pink and blue!

Accompaniment

8va sempre

A snooker puzzle

In snooker:

Draw a circle around a musical note that counts:

A red ball counts as **one**

as **one** ♩ ♩. 𝅝

A yellow ball counts as **two**

as **two** 𝅝 ♩ ♪

A green ball counts as **three**

as **three** 𝅗𝅥. 𝅝 ♩

A brown ball counts as **four**

as **four** 𝅗𝅥 ♩ 𝅝

What's your score?

There are four snooker balls in each box. Can you write their notes in the next box and then add up the score?
The first one has been done for you.

| ♩ 𝅗𝅥. 𝅝 𝅗𝅥 | = | 10 |

| | = | |

| | = | |

Snowman

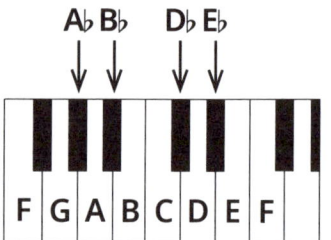

Coolly

The snow - man stands in the gar - den with snow right up to his knees:___

___ why won't he come in and warm him - self? He says he'd ra - ther freeze!

Accompaniment

8va sempre *Staccato, like snowflakes*

Clowns

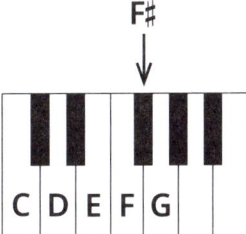

Playfully

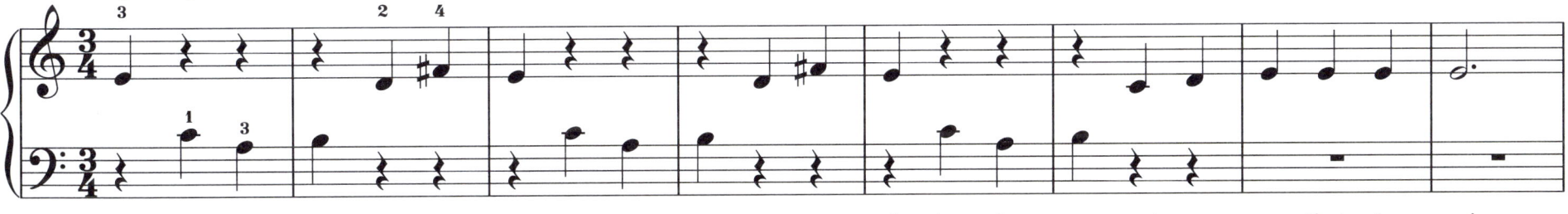

Here comes a clown wear-ing big bag-gy trou-sers, a wig that is green and a nose that is red.

Here comes his friend with a buck-et of cus-tard, and cheer-ful-ly tips it all o-ver his head.

Accompaniment

When you have played all the pieces in this book, choose the three that you like best.

Write their names here, then play them a lot until you really know them!

1.
2.
3.

Why don't you play them to someone and give them a treat?

2 04